Easy & Elegant
CHRISTMAS TREES

Easy & Elegant CHRISTMAS TREES

CLAIRE WORTHINGTON

Text by Emma Callery

Checkmark
Books

For Charlie

Easy & Elegant Christmas Trees

Copyright © Collins & Brown Limited 1998
Text copyright © Collins & Brown Ltd 1998
Illustrations copyright © Collins & Brown Ltd 1998
Photographs copyright © Collins & Brown Ltd 1998

First published in Great Britain in 1998 by Collins & Brown Limited

Checkmark Books
An imprint of Facts On File, Inc.
11 Penn Plaza
New York NY 10001

Library of Congress Cataloging-in-Publication Data
Worthington, Claire.
     Easy & elegant Christmas trees : 30 projects with step-by-step
instructions / Claire Worthington : text by Emma Callery.
          p. cm
     Includes index.
     ISBN 0-8160-3864-3
     1. Christmas decorations.   2. Handicraft.   3. Christmas trees.
I. Callery. Emma.   II. Title.
TT900 .C4W67 1998
745.594'12–dc21

Facts On File books are available at special discounts when purchased in bulk quantities for businesses, associations, institutions or sales promotions. Please call our Special Sales Department in New York at (212) 967-800 or (800) 322-8755.

You can find Facts On File on the World Wide Web at http://www.factsonfile.com

Conceived, edited and designed by Collins & Brown Limited

Editor: Emma Callery
Designer: Roger Daniels
Style photography: Jacqui Hurst
Step-by-step photography: Shona Wood
Cutout photography: Matthew Dickens
Additional picture credits: page 128

Reproduction by Graphiscan
Printed in Mexico

10 9 8 7 6 5 4 3 2 1

This book is printed on acid-free paper.

Contents

INTRODUCTION

One of the greatest of traditions at Christmas is decorating the tree. Choosing your tree and bringing it home; finding the right pot to stand it in, and then covering it with decorations never fails to entertain. As for turning on the lights for the first time, this is a truly magical moment. This book is a celebration of the Christmas tree with seven different styles of tree and 30 original projects for you to decorate your tree with. The projects are simple to make, all the materials used are readily available and no special tools are needed. All children love helping to decorate the tree and many of these ideas are suitable for small fingers to make. The decorations you produce can be carefully packed away at the end of the festive season and rediscovered year after year.

The history of the Christmas tree is surprisingly long and there are a great number of traditional stories associated with it. The earliest 'trees' were palms that the early Egyptians brought indoors as symbols of eternal life while ancient Jewish religious feasts used decorations made from tree boughs. But it was the Romans who exchanged boughs and greenery for trees. These were paraded with candles and trinkets attached to the branches to celebrate the winter festival of Saturnalia. Druid priests decorated oak trees with golden apples for their winter solstice festivities. These stories pre-date the life of Jesus, but the links with Christianity became increasingly strong over the following centuries.

It is said that Martin Luther introduced the tree tradition to Germany early in the sixteenth century. He was walking on a star-lit night, pondering the birth of Christ, when he became enthralled by the surrounding evergreen trees

nestling among the snowy landscape. He took a tree inside and decorated it with candles to recreate the majesty he felt about Christ's birth. By 1531, Christmas trees were on sale in Strasburg's market place and were taken into homes for the holiday period. They remained undecorated, however, and it was only later

that they became increasingly ornamented in Germany using paper flowers, fruits, nuts, gold foil, cakes, small gifts and candies. From Germany, the tradition of bringing a tree inside at Christmas to be decorated spread to America and England during the nineteenth century.

It is accepted that it was Queen Victoria's consort, Prince Albert, who first introduced the Christmas tree to Britain in 1841. He had a lighted tree set up in Windsor Castle so that he could re-live his happy childhood memories in Germany. However, there are records of German immigrant workers in Manchester bringing trees into their homes by 1822. Nevertheless, it was Prince Albert who popularized the elaborately decorated tree and there are many Victorian paintings and drawings showing the Christmas tree being brought home through the snow indicating just how important a ceremony this ancient tradition became at that time, and remains to this today.

German mercenaries first took the idea to America: in 1804, US soldiers stationed at Fort Dearborn (now Chicago) hauled trees from surrounding woods

to their barracks at Christmas. The first tree was sold on a sidewalk in New York City in 1851 and the fame of the Christmas tree soon spread.

The first American President to proudly display his Christmas tree at the White House was Franklin Pierce in 1856, and in 1889 Benjamin Harrison announced that his White House tree was now part of an American tradition. This paved the way for the huge growth of the Christmas tree market although there was a minor backlash in the 1930s when Theodore Roosevelt announced that, for the sake of forest conservation, the White House would no longer have a tree. Somewhat embarrassingly for their father, however, his two sons quietly put a small tree in their room.

Armed with all this information, you can now look at your Christmas tree in quite a different light. This book contains a wealth of ideas to inspire you to go ahead and decorate your tree, in the knowledge that millions of people have done this over many hundreds of years.

Tree of Treats

Food is an important part of Christmas celebrations and this glittering tree is laden with easy-to-make, yet delicious, edible treats. There are meringue mice with almond ears, cookies cut into festive shapes and decorated with silver drops, iridescent bags of sugared almonds tied with organza ribbon and stenciled papers to wrap around biscuits.

This is a tree that the whole family can have a great time decorating. Children can have enormous fun cutting out and decorating the cookies; and they will enjoy icing the meringue mice and popping on their ears eyes and noses. These are extremely appealing as each face looks different. Making almond bags and tying them with ribbons are tasks done best by older children.

A tree decorated like this looks wonderful and its treats taste even better, so you will have to keep an eye on family and friends to ensure all the goodies aren't eaten before Christmas is over.

TREATS *Gallery*

Left: ORGANZA RIBBON AND WHITE
TISSUE PAPER MAKE LOVELY
WRAPPERS FOR DELICIOUS
AMARETTO COOKIES.

Below: IRIDESCENT TRANSLUCENT
CELLOPHANE IS AVAILABLE IN ALL
MANNER OF COLORS, BUT PINK, BLUE
AND CREAM ARE THE BEST TO LOOK
FOR AS THEY SO BEAUTIFULLY
COMPLEMENT THEIR CONTENTS: A
HANDFUL OF SUGARED ALMONDS.

Above: SMALL COOKIES HUNG ON SILVER THREAD HAVE ADDED SPARKLE WHEN EDIBLE SILVER BALLS ARE STUCK ONTO THEM TO MAKE PATTERNS.

Left: MERINGUE MICE NESTLE AMONG THE BRANCHES OF THIS CHRISTMAS TREE, JUST WAITING TO BE POUNCED UPON.

$\mathcal{M}$ERINGUE MICE

Meringue is best cooked at a low temperature for 2 hours so make sure you have plenty of time ahead of you.

YOU WILL NEED

MAKES ABOUT 16

4 EGG WHITES
(AT ROOM
TEMPERATURE)

8OZ (225G)
WHITE SUGAR

BAKING TRAY

GREASEPROOF PAPER

ICING BAG

PALETTE KNIFE

EDIBLE SILVER BALLS

PEPPERCORNS

SPLIT ALMONDS

BRADAWL

GOLD WIRE STRING

PREPARATION

Place the egg whites in a large bowl and whisk at high speed until soft peaks form. Add the sugar, 1 tsp at a time, whisking well each time.

1

Line the baking tray with greaseproof paper and heat the oven to 200°F/100°C/ gas mark ½. Then spoon the mixture into a icing bag and squeeze wedge shapes on the greaseproof paper.

2

Smooth the shapes into small mice-like bodies using the palette knife. Keep back some of the icing for step 4.

3

To make the mice faces, add silver balls for the noses, peppercorns for the eyes (don't forget to remove these before eating!), and split almonds for the ears.

4

Bake in the oven for about 2 hours or until very slightly golden. Cool and then use the bradawl to poke a small hole for the tail. Add the gold wire string for the tail, fastening it with uncooked meringue.

SUGARED ALMOND BAGS

Small fingers will love filling these bags with sugared almonds, but tying the tops can be tricky so is best done by an adult.

YOU WILL NEED

IRIDESCENT CELLOPHANE

SCISSORS

CLEAR STICKY TAPE

SUGARED ALMONDS

ORGANZA RIBBON

GOLD STRING

1

Cut out pieces of iridescent cellophane about 6in (15cm) square.

2

Stick each piece of cellophane together in the middle and then at one end as if tying a parcel.

3

Fill each bag with sugared almonds. Don't put too many almonds into each bag as they are quite heavy and will weigh the tree down too much.

4

Tie each bag at the top with a piece of organza ribbon. To attach the bag to the tree catch a piece of gold string into the ribbon as you tie it.

Tree of Treats

FESTIVE COOKIES

Edible silver balls are very attractive decorations and can be used for all sorts of patterns and pictures on these pretty cookies.

YOU WILL NEED

4OZ (110G) BUTTER

2OZ (50G) WHITE SUGAR

GRATED RIND OF ONE LEMON

5OZ (150G) PLAIN FLOUR

ROLLING PIN

VARIETY OF CUTTERS

GREASEPROOF PAPER

BAKING TRAY

EDIBLE SILVER BALLS

BRADAWL

SILVER STRING

1

Mix all the ingredients together in a mixer. Heat the oven to 240°F/180°C/gas mark 4 and roll out the pastry on a floured surface.

2

Cut out a variety of shapes using the cookie cutters. Try to cut as many as possible from the pastry so that you don't have to roll it out too frequently.

3

Lay the cookies on a piece of greaseproof paper on a baking tray and decorate with the edible silver balls.

4

Make a hole in each cookie with the bradawl before putting them in the oven for 10 minutes until pale brown. Once cooked, cool on a wire rack, and thread the holes with silver string.

AMARETTO WRAPPERS

YOU WILL NEED

STENCIL TEMPLATES ON PAGES 120-121

STENCIL CARD CUT TO THE SIZE OF THE FINISHED WRAPPERS

PENCIL

EXACTO OR CRAFT KNIFE

CUTTING MAT

TISSUE PAPER

PEBBLES

GOLD SPRAY PAINT

ROUGH PAPER

ORGANZA RIBBON

1

Using the templates on pages 120-121 or one of your own (perhaps copy a design from a Christmas card or wrapping paper), transfer the design on to stencil card. Simple geometric designs work best.

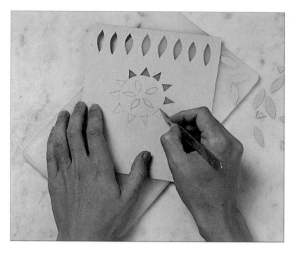

2

On a cutting mat, carefully cut out the design with the exacto or craft knife.

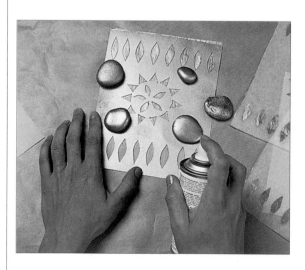

3

Cut pieces of tissue paper to the same size as the card. Lay the card over the tissue paper, on rough paper to protect your worksurface, and use pebbles to hold it in place. Lightly spray with gold spray paint.

4

When the paint is dry, wrap each cookie or sweet in a stenciled paper and tie the ends with organza ribbon.

Colorful Tree

In Christian areas of India, jewel-bright colors are used to festoon Christmas trees. In addition, very colorful stars are put over the trees' lights to add to the effect. Here is a tree reminiscent of this look, with red, purple, blue and yellow enhanced with shimmering gold and shining sequins.

All of the objects on this tree can be made quickly and simply and require very few materials and just a little know-how. The baubles, for example, are strips of tissue paper folded over small Styrofoam balls, held in place with glue. A variety of designs can then be made with braids and brightly colored ribbons: keep an eye out throughout the year for scraps that can be used creatively in this way. Only small pieces are needed at a time. Likewise, the stars are made from small pieces of fabric; here silk dupioni has been used which has a luster all its own. But many other shiny fabrics are also available and, as only such small pieces are used, a remnant or two would be quite sufficient.

COLORFUL *Gallery*

Left and below left:
IT IS THE DETAILS THAT COUNT.
HERE SHINY SEQUINS AND GOLD
TASSELS ADORN SIMPLE OBJECTS,
TURNING THEM INTO SOMETHING
EVEN MORE COLORFUL.

Above and left: ON A COLORFUL
CHRISTMAS TREE SUCH AS THIS ONE,
THERE IS NO NEED TO WORRY ABOUT
CLASHING SHADES. BLUES AND REDS
SIT NEXT TO PURPLES, PINKS AND
YELLOWS MORE THAN HAPPILY. THE
END-RESULT IS AN ENERGETIC MIX.

$\mathcal{B}$RAIDED BAUBLES

Braids, ribbons and sequins are quickly and simply held in place with dressmakers' pins making this project very versatile.

1

Cut out strips of tissue paper that are long and wide enough to wrap around the Styrofoam balls.

2

Wrap the tissue paper around the balls and glue into place at the top and bottom with the rubber-based glue.

3

Wind the gold cord around each ball to make whatever pattern you want. Use the dressmakers' pins to invisibly secure it, gluing the pin in place to prevent it falling out accidentally.

4

Embellish further using fancy braid. Here the braid overlaps alternate strands of the cord, but there are many other ways in which you can use it (see opposite for some further ideas).

Colorful Tree

ABRIC STAR

The brighter the fabric the better. Any colorful material will do, but the two-way colors of silk dupioni add style.

YOU WILL NEED

TEMPLATE ON PAGE 124

STIFF CARD

SCISSORS

FABRIC PENCIL OR CHALK

SELECTION OF COLORED SILK DUPIONI

NEEDLE

THREAD

WADDING

BEADS, SEQUINS AND BRAIDS

SMALL GLASS BEADS

1

Transfer the template from page 124 onto a piece of stiff card and cut out. Draw around it onto the pieces of fabric (two for each star) using the fabric pencil or chalk. Then cut out the stars.

2

Join together two stars of different colors with right sides facing. Stitch together by hand or with a machine, leaving a small gap for turning through. Turn right sides out and then stuff with wadding.

3

If necessary, poke out the corners with a small pair of scissors as you stuff. Turn in the final opening and sew it up by hand with tiny overstitches.

4

Embellish the stars with beads, sequins and braids (see opposite for more decorative ideas). For a final twinkle, sew small glass beads onto each point and then hang the stars on the tree.

  *Colorful Tree*

PAPERCHAINS

One of the most popular of children's decorations at Christmas, here is a glitzy version to add some glamor.

YOU WILL NEED

ROUGH PAPER

GOLD CRAFT PAPER

GOLD SPRAY PAINT

RULER

PENCIL

SCISSORS

SEQUINS

ALL-PURPOSE GLUE

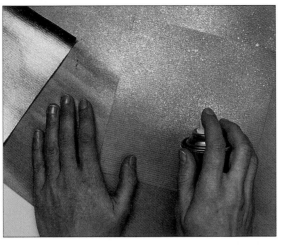

1

Protect your worksurface with rough paper. Spray the back of your gold paper with gold paint so that the insides of the paperchains will glimmer just like the outsides once they are hanging on the tree.

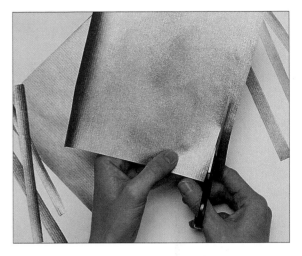

2

Mark faint guidelines approximately ½in (1cm) apart on the paper with a ruler and pencil and then cut the paper into strips.

3

For some added sparkle, on the outside of each strip, stick a sequin in the middle and at one end.

4

Link the strips together, gluing the ends, to make one very long chain or several shorter ones to drape all over the tree.

Colorful Tree

$\mathcal{T}$REE BAG

Silk dupioni is available in the brightest of colors: choose shades that complement each other and the rest of the tree's decor.

YOU WILL NEED

SILK DUPIONI IN
TWO COLORS

TAPE MEASURE

FABRIC CHALK
OR PENCIL

SCISSORS

NEEDLE

COTTON THREAD

PINS

BRAIDS

RICK-RACK BRAID

STRING OF SILVER
SEQUINS

FANCY CORD

2 TASSELS

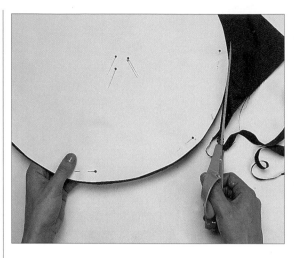

1

Cut a 14in (35cm) diameter circle from one piece of silk, and two rectangles measuring 14×43in (35×110cm) and 4×43in (10×110cm) from the other.

2

Stitch together the narrow ends with right sides facing. Then, still with right sides facing, stitch the wider circle to the base, and the narrower one (folded in half wrong sides together) to the top edge.

3

Trim the seams and turn right sides out. Then embellish the bag using braids, rick-rack braid and sequins on strings.

4

Make a small opening in the drawstring pocket and thread the cord through it by pinning a safety pin onto one end of the cord to pull it through. To finish, sew a tassel onto each end of the cord.

Country Tree

Bring the outside in with decorations that incorporate the best that nature provides. Woody tones and earthy shades abound with a collection of diverse objects: cinnamon sticks and cloves for a gentle spicy perfume; nuts and pomegranates for their rippled and nobbly surfaces; dried leaves wired together to form exotic blooms, and a twig star for the tree's crowning glory. For added lift, gold has been put to good use on this tree in the form of gilt cream on the cinnamon bundles and nutmeg leaves, spray paint on the pine cones and other seed pods, and liquid leaf on the pomegranates.

The perfect container for a country-styled tree is a plain terracotta pot that reflects the earthy tones of the decorations. Here the container has been filled to bursting with huge pine cones, which can be collected throughout the autumn and look wonderful when piled high. Nature's bounty can really be made the most of when it is dried like this: it is just begging to come into the warmth.

COUNTRY *Gallery*

Left and right:
NATURAL TONES
WITH ADDED
SPARKLE FOR A
COUNTRY TREE
THAT WANTS TO
SHINE.

Right:
HEAVILY
TEXTURED
TWIGS THAT
ARE WIRED
TOGETHER IN
A SIMPLE STAR
SHAPE LOOK
EVEN BETTER
WHEN SMALL
FLOWER HEADS
ARE WIRED IN
PLACE.

Left and below: NUTS AND FRUITS HAVE BEEN BROUGHT INDOORS TO GARNISH THIS TREE. DECORATED WITH HINTS OF GOLD OR ADORNED WITH LIGHTLY SCENTED CLOVES, THE TEXTURAL MIX IS WIDE-RANGING.

CINNAMON BUNDLES

Simple to make, these bundles are especially effective when hung all over the tree.

YOU WILL NEED

CINNAMON STICKS

CRAFT KNIFE

RAFFIA

GILT CREAM

1

Cut the pieces of cinnamon into lengths of about 2in (5cm).

2

Group the cut sticks into fours and then tie the pieces together using a few strands of raffia.

3

Tie the raffia ends together close to the bundle to secure, and then again further away from the cinnamon sticks to form a hanging loop.

4

Rub the part of the raffia that is tied around each cinnamon bundle with the gilt cream.

TWIGGY STAR

For the best effect, gather twigs that are nobbly and lichen-encrusted: the texture adds a lot to the end result.

YOU WILL NEED

COLLECTION OF TWIGS

FLORISTS' WIRE

GOLD SPRAY PAINT

ROUGH PAPER

DRIED FLOWER HEADS

1

Cut short lengths of twig from the branches you have gathered. You will need six twigs for each star. Make two triangles by wiring the twigs together at the points.

2

Fit the two triangles together to create the star shape and wire together, as before. One triangle can sit on top of the other or you can weave the points together.

3

Protect your worksurface with rough paper. For an icy effect, spray gold paint over the star in patches. Don't spray on too much or the subtle effect will be lost.

4

For added decoration, wire the small dried flower heads all over the star. The muted shades of dried flowers look especially good against wood.

NUTMEG LEAVES

You can either make your own glycerined beech leaves or buy them ready-prepared from a florist.

YOU WILL NEED

NUTMEGS

FLORISTS' WIRE

CLEAR STICKY TAPE

GILT CREAM

GLYCERINED BEECH LEAVES

1

Stick a piece of wire onto the bottom of each nutmeg using small pieces of the sticky tape.

2

Rub the nutmegs lightly with some gilt cream, letting some of the natural color of the nuts show through.

3

Attach a short length of florists' wire onto several glycerined beech leaves to bundle them together.

4

Group several sets of beech leaves with each wired nutmeg and twist all the wires together to form a flower shape.

 TOUCH OF GOLD

There are many ways to add hints of gold to decorative objects. Here are three of the most straightforward.

YOU
WILL
NEED

SELECTION OF CONES
AND SEED PODS

GOLD SPRAY PAINT

GOLD STRING

DRIED
POMEGRANATES

LIQUID LEAF PAINT

ARTISTS' PAINTBRUSH

BRADAWL

FLORISTS' WIRE

TACKS

ALL-PURPOSE GLUE

WALNUTS

GILT CREAM

SPRAY PAINT

1

Spray a selection of pine cones and other seed pods with gold paint.

2

Tie a piece of gold string onto the end of each bundle for hanging.

LIQUID LEAF

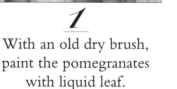

1

With an old dry brush, paint the pomegranates with liquid leaf.

2

Make a hole with bradawl. Wind wire around tack, and glue tack in hole.

GILT CREAM

1

Rub walnuts with gilt cream, letting the nuts' texture show through.

2

Fasten a wired tack in a hole in each base as in Step 2, above.

Children's Tree

Children love bright colors and sparkly objects, so if you have young children around at Chistmas time dress your tree like this and you are bound to please them. The felt stars and birds are made with very simple stitches so older children will find the instructions given on pages 56 and 66 satisfyingly easy to follow.

The card Christmas trees will appeal to the younger maker. Although the sequins have been stuck in a regular pattern for the photographs in this book, there is, of course, no reason why they can't be applied in a more haphazard manner as would befit experimenting four-year-olds. For a spot of variety, glitter pens can also be used very creatively and work as well.

The advent tags are a wonderful way to count down to the big day; they should be made by an adult though as they are more tricky to make. Hang them on a wall before the Christmas tree is brought in.

CHILDREN'S *Gallery*

Above: BRIGHTLY
COLORED FELT BIRDS
HOVER AMONG THE
BRANCHES OF THE
TREE.

Right: A COUNTDOWN
TO CHRISTMAS.
BEHIND EACH
NUMBERED DOOR IS A
PICTURE; THE PERFECT
WAY FOR A CHILD TO
MARK TIME.

Above: SIMPLICITY ITSELF – TWO
DECORATED PIECES OF CARD
SLOTTED TOGETHER MAKE A
CHARMINGLY NAIVE DECORATION.

Left: THE SOFTNESS OF FELT IS
ENDURINGLY ALLURING TO A
CHILD. IT IS ALSO INCREDIBLY
EASY TO WORK WITH, SO IS A
PERFECT CHILD-FRIENDLY
MATERIAL.

ELT BIRDS

The beauty of felt is that there are no fraying edges to contend with. Cut out your shapes and they will remain the same.

YOU WILL NEED

TEMPLATES ON PAGE 59

COLORED FELT

SCISSORS

RUBBER-BASED GLUE

ARTISTS' PAINTBRUSH

NEEDLE

COLORED EMBROIDERY THREADS

WADDING

BLUE GLASS BEADS

1

Using the templates on page 59, cut out a square of felt, the color that you would like the bird's body to be. Cut out the tail pieces and wings from other colors. Cut a small triangle of yellow felt for the beak.

2

Stick the beak onto one corner of the body using the rubber-based adhesive.

3

Fold the square over into a triangle and, starting from the end with the beak, sew the two edges together using herringbone stitch in a contrasting colored embroidery thread.

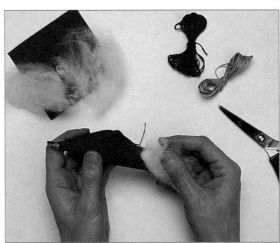

4

When you have about 1¼in (3cm) left to stitch, stuff the bird with the wadding. Do not sew the opening closed.

5

Roll two different colored tail pieces together.

6

Push the straight end of the tail piece into the body through the hole where the wadding was stuffed and stitch in place to secure.

7

Attach the wings using a contrasting colored thread and then embellish the middle of the wing with an embroidered sunburst shape.

8

Sew on small glass beads as eyes and attach a loop of thread to the bird's back for hanging it from the tree.

  *Children's Tree*

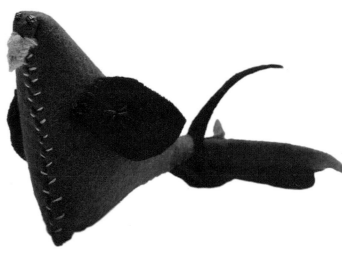

Body (cut 1)

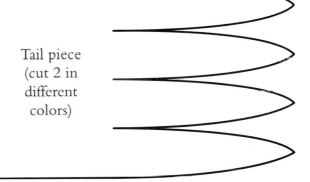

Tail piece
(cut 2 in
different
colors)

Wings (cut 2)

A

DVENT TAGS

The backing card for these tags is red but you could also use Christmas paper, as long as it is fairly stiff.

YOU WILL NEED

TEMPLATE ON PAGE 63

GOLD PAPER

SCISSORS

EXACTO

RED CARD

PENCIL

PICTURE STICKERS

ALL-PURPOSE GLUE

SEQUINS

GLITTER PEN

GOLD STRING

1

Using the template from page 63, draw 24 shapes onto the gold paper.

2

Roughly cut out the shapes so that you can tell approximately how large they will be when the tags are finished.

3

Using the scalpel and a template, on each tag cut out the door on three sides.

4

For the backs, draw around the template 24 times onto the red card and cut out roughly. On the reverse side of the card, mark where the doors are to go with the pencil and template.

Children's Tree

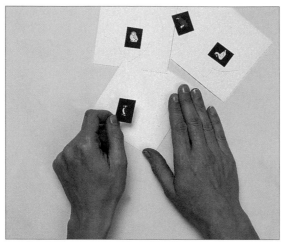

5

Cut out small squares of red card marginally bigger than the size of the door. Fasten on a sticker and glue the whole thing over the area marked for the door.

6

Stick the fronts and backs together taking care not to glue the door shut. Cut out around the line originally marked on the gold paper.

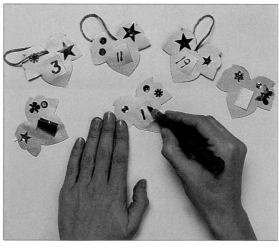

7

Embellish each tag liberally with sequins, fastening them in place with the all-purpose glue.

8

Using the glitter pen, number the tags from 1 to 24. Make a small hole with an exacto at the top of each tag and thread with gold string.

  *Children's Tree*

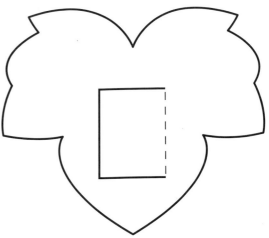

The tag template
(cut out 24 in gold paper and 24 in card)

ELT STAR

The embroidery stitches used for this project are straightforward, making the star ideal for a child to make.

YOU WILL NEED

TEMPLATES ON
PAGE 124

GREEN AND RED
FELT

WADDING

NEEDLE

RED AND GREEN
EMBROIDERY
THREADS

RED, GOLD AND
GREEN BEADS

1

Cut out the felt using the templates on page 124. Use red for the front, and green for the back and the small star on the front.

2

Sew the small green star on to the front of the red one using small overstitches and red embroidery thread. Then embellish it with red and gold beads (see the picture opposite for a suggested design).

3

Sew a ½in- (1cm-) wide strip of felt onto the back star, attaching it at both ends with neat overstitches to form a loop by which to attach the star to the top of the tree.

4

Sew the two sides of the star together using blanket stitch and lightly pad it with wadding as you go. Thread a bead onto the thread every third stitch or so, alternating the colors in a regular pattern.

CHRISTMAS TREES

Usually these small trees are made to stand on a table, but here they are made to be hung by loops from the tree.

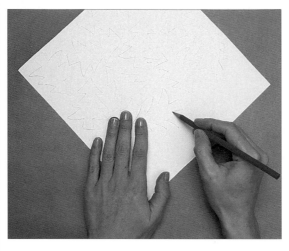

1

Draw around the template on page 71 several times onto a piece of the white card (each tree needs two cut-outs).

2

Protect your worksurface with rough paper. Evenly spray across the back of the card with the gold paint.

3

Carefully cut out each tree. For the neatest finish it is best to cut into each branch from the outside edge. Working in and out down the side can result in a bent card.

4

Evenly coat the white sides with the silver spray paint.

 *Children's Tree*

  Children's Tree

5

Embellish the point of each branch – and on both sides – with the red and green sequins. You may choose to alternate the colors, as here, or use just one color on each tree.

6

Cut half the tree shapes vertically down the middle, starting at the top, to slightly over the halfway point. Then, starting at the bottom, cut the other half of the tree shapes in the same way.

7

Slide the two halves together. Pierce the top of the tree with a needle, thread some fishing line through the hole and tie it together to form a loop.

Christmas tree template

White Tree

The noble fir tree is extremely elegant when decked with silver decorations and covered lightly with spray snow. The end result is beautifully crisp and frosty. Using only white to decorate a Christmas tree has a classic, timeless appeal and here the idea has been developed subtly to include a lot of silver and glass. The reflective qualities of these surfaces are quite wonderful, combining with the fairy lights for an overall soft shimmer.

The main material that has been used for the decorations on this tree is aluminum foil. By carefully snipping out shapes and indenting patterns, the end results look very professional. The main tools that are needed to recreate them are an old pair of scissors and a ballpoint pen – implements that are in every household. For added sparkle, glass beads, glitter and sequins have been stuck to the decorations. To complete the setting, many snowflake chains cascade down the wall behind the tree.

WHITE *Gallery*

Right: ALUMINUM AND GLASS ARE
COMBINED TO MAKE A
FUTURISTIC-LOOKING BAUBLE.
THE SHINY SURFACES AND MULTI-
FACETED PRONGS GIVE IT THE AIR
OF A TECHNO-SNOWFLAKE.

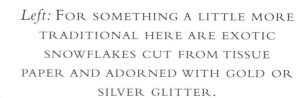

Left: FOR SOMETHING A LITTLE MORE
TRADITIONAL HERE ARE EXOTIC
SNOWFLAKES CUT FROM TISSUE
PAPER AND ADORNED WITH GOLD OR
SILVER GLITTER.

White Tree

This page:
IMPRINTING
PATTERNS ON
ALUMINUM FOIL
WITH A
BALLPOINT PEN
CREATES A
RAISED FINISH.
THE FOIL CAN
THEN BE
MANIPULATED
INTO ALL
MANNER OF
CHRISTMAS
ORNAMENTS.

*I*CICLES

The aluminum foil that is used for this project and for others later in the book is special foil, see page 128 for a mail-order supplier.

YOU WILL NEED

TEMPLATES ON PAGE 126

PENCIL

GREASEPROOF PAPER

SCISSORS

ALUMINUM FOIL

CLEAR STICKY TAPE

BALLPOINT PEN

GLASS BEADS

FISHING LINE

RUBBER-BASED GLUE

1

Trace the templates on page 126 onto a piece of greaseproof paper and roughly cut around the outlines.

2

Stick the tracing onto the aluminum foil using clear sticky tape and draw over the detailed patterns using the ballpoint pen. Press hard.

3

Cut out the shapes from the aluminum foil but don't use your best scissors!

4

Roll each of the parts into a cone shape and carefully stick them together on the inside using small pieces of clear sticky tape.

White Tree

 5

Take a piece of fishing line, tie a knot at one end and then thread some glass beads onto it. Thread the other end of the line through the point of the largest cone. Fasten on the inside using sticky tape.

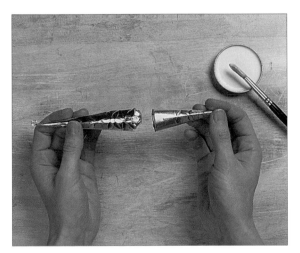

6

Take a small piece of paper and screw it up into a ball. Then glue both parts of the icicle onto the paper so that the larger piece of foil overlaps the smaller.

S NOWFLAKES

These glittery snowflakes look wonderful strung together or placed individually on the tree lights.

1

Cut out small circles of silver tissue paper. These can be all the same size or varying, depending on the effect you desire.

2

Fold each circle into eight by folding in half, in half again, and then in half one more time.

3

Snip a pattern into each piece of tissue (remember that every snowflake is different). Make the pattern as intricate as you like but don't cut folds away completely or the flake will fall to pieces.

4

Embellish with glitter stuck on to glue. Do this on scrap paper to catch the glitter for recyling. If using the flakes on the lights, switch off and push the flakes well down the outsides of the plastic casings.

$\mathcal{T}$IN STARS

This is the perfect project for young fingers: tracing and using glitter are always very popular pursuits.

YOU
WILL
NEED

TEMPLATE ON
PAGE 124

PENCIL

GREASEPROOF PAPER

ALUMINUM FOIL

CLEAR STICKY TAPE

BALLPOINT PEN

SCISSORS

WHITE CARD

RUBBER-BASED GLUE

GOLD GLITTER

FISHING LINE

1

Trace the template on pager 124 onto a piece of greaseproof paper. Stick the tracing onto the aluminum foil using clear sticky tape and draw over the design with the ballpoint pen. Press hard.

2

Carefully cut out each star with the scissors (not your best pair as they will be blunted).

3

Using a tin star as a template, draw around the star onto pieces of white card, allowing a ¼in (5mm) margin around the tin. Spread glue all over the card backings and stick the tin stars in the center.

4

Sprinkle the card surround with glitter. If you do this over a piece of paper it will be easier to tip excess glitter back into the tube to be used again. Dust off excess and thread with fishing line for a loop.

*T*IN ANGEL

This is the longest project in this book; but don't be deterred. Although care needs to be taken, the end result is worth it.

1

Trace the wings, sleeves, crown and skirt templates onto greaseproof paper and roughly cut out the shapes. Stick onto aluminum foil, and draw firmly over the outlines and details with the ballpoint pen.

2

Cut the angel's body from a piece of florists' foam. The finished piece looks like a pyramid with the top sliced off, and the base measures 1¼ × 1in (3 × 2cm).

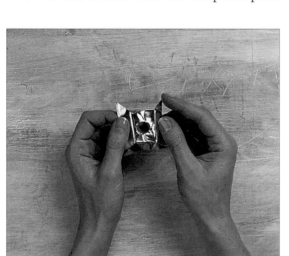

3

Cut out a small rectangular piece of aluminum foil and make a hole in the center. Then use the foil to cover the top of the florists' foam body.

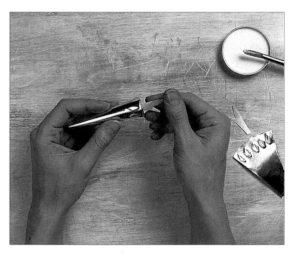

4

Cut out the prepared sleeves from the foil, roll into cones and fasten on the inside with sticky tape. Cut the hands (see page 123) from the gold paper and stick with adhesive into the wide end of the sleeves.

5

Draw the face like that on page 123 onto a small oval-shaped piece of gold paper and stick onto the candle. Pare the candle down slightly with a sharp knife if the one you have is too large.

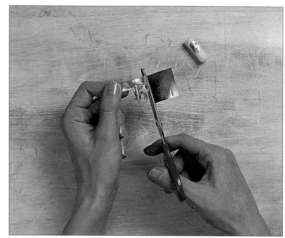

6

To make the angel's hair, cut out a small rectangular piece of foil and snip along one edge, as shown on page 123. Stick the hair around the candle with the face on it, ensuring that the fringe is at the front.

7

Cut out the prepared crown from the aluminum foil and stick over the hair with the rubber-based glue.

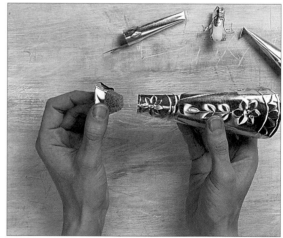

8

Cut out the prepared skirt, roll into a cone and fasten on the inside with sticky tape. Then stick the body and the skirt together using the rubber-based glue.

White Tree

9

For the top part of the angel's dress, wind a string of silver sequins around the body. Start from the waist and work upwards, gluing the sequins into place at the top.

10

Flatten the top of the sleeve cones and fold over ¼in (5mm) to make a hinge. Slot the hinges into the top of the body between the sequins and florists' foam.

11

Add the head, pushing the bottom of the candle (covered with glue) firmly into the hole made in the foil and through into the florists' foam.

12

Cut out the prepared wings from the aluminum foil and stick them to the back of the angel with the rubber-based glue. The top of the wings should be aligned about half way up her head.

ℬEADED BAUBLES

Dressmakers' pins are available in different lengths. For this project it is best to use the longest you can find.

YOU WILL NEED

STYROFOAM BALLS IN ASSORTED SIZES

SILVER TISSUE PAPER

SCISSORS

RUBBER-BASED GLUE

SMALL CYLINDRICAL GLASS BEADS

SMALL PLAIN GLASS BEADS

SILVER SEQUINS

DRESSMAKERS' PINS

ALL-PURPOSE GLUE

FISHING LINE

1

Cut out rectangles of aluminum foil large enough to wrap around the Styrofoam balls.

2

Thread three cylindrical glass sleeves, a plain glass bead and a silver sequin onto a dressmakers' pin.

3

Dip the pointed end of the decorated pin into the adhesive. Then push it into the covered Styrofoam ball as far as possible so that none of the uncovered pin shows.

4

Repeat steps 2 and 3 until the whole ball is covered. Add some fishing line in a loop for hanging from the tree. Fasten the fishing line to the ball with a pin stuck in place as before.

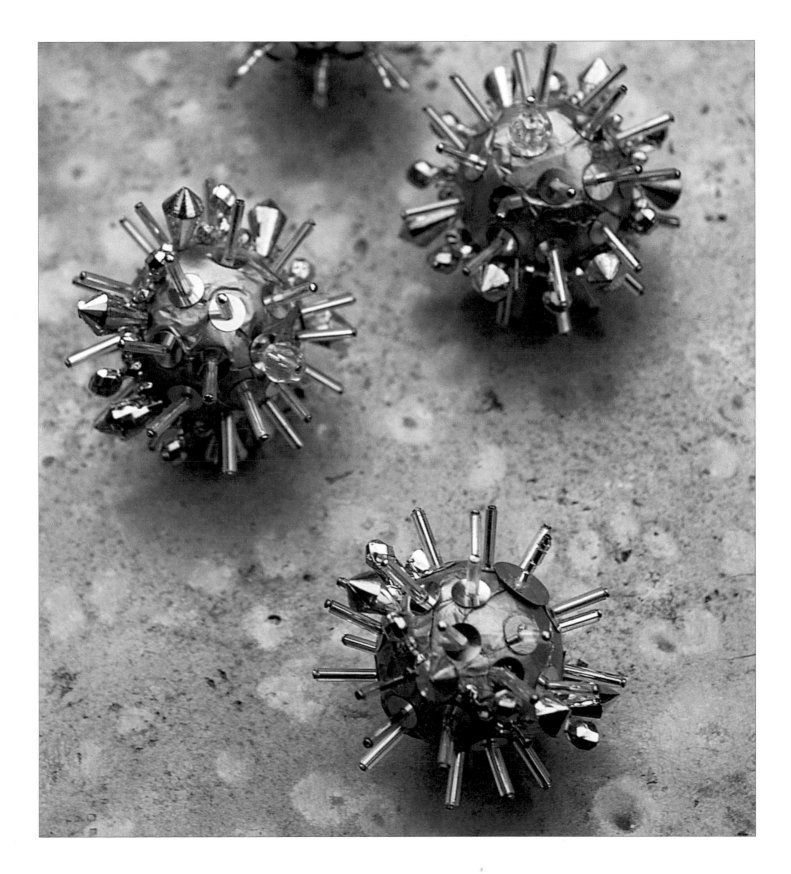

Table Tree

Here is the perfect tree if you don't have sufficient space for a full-size one, or if you want to add a little extra decoration somewhere else in the home. Instead of the traditional Norwegian spruce evergreen, a clipped box tree has been put in a small terracotta pot – the perfect scale of tree to stand on a table top or dresser.

Decorating such a small tree requires restraint and, of course, not too many pieces or it will start to look over-whelmed. Fairy lights, too, would look a little out of place so they have been left off. Instead, to add that touch of sparkle and festivity that is so necessary on a Christmas tree, the box tree has been decorated with plenty of exotic gold – of the fake variety. The gold-embellished Chinese lanterns look just like stars peeping out from between the branches, and the candles at its foot glimmer next to the pot. The moss and kumquats resting on top of the pot add just the right note: nature at its best and in miniature.

TABLE *Gallery*

Right and below: FAKE GOLD LEAF IS A
BEAUTIFUL ADDITION TO CHRISTMAS
TREE DECORATIONS, ESPECIALLY
WHEN COMBINED WITH GOLD. IT HAS
A LUXURIOUS GLOW AND A HINT OF
EXTRAVAGANCE.

Right: AS A LITTLE
EXTRA, KUMQUATS
WRAPPED WITH
GOLD CORD AND
STUDDED WITH
CLOVES NESTLE
AMONG PLAIN
KUMQUATS IN A
GOLD-EMBOSSED
BOWL.

Left: THIS LONG CACHE POT
HAS BEEN COVERED WITH
FAKE GOLD LEAF TO ADD A
GLOWING FINISHING TOUCH
TO THE TREE'S STAND.

MINIATURE POMANDERS

These oval kumquats make for very unusually shaped pomanders. Their size also complements a small tree.

1

Tie a piece of gold thread around the kumquats to divide them into quarters. Anchor with dressmakers' pins if necessary.

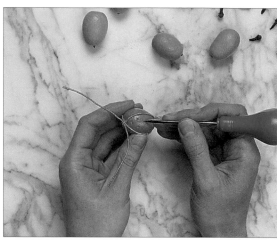

2

Poke holes all over the kumquats with a bradawl or other pointed implement.

3

Insert the cloves into the holes, pushing them in as far as they will go.

4

To use the pomanders as a moth deterrent, repeat steps 1 to 3, but using ordinary string. Sprinkle with sieved orrisroot and leave in an airing cupboard for two weeks. Then replace the string with gold thread.

GILDED CHINESE LANTERNS

Gold and orange combine very well, but fake silver leaf is also available and you might like to consider a mixture or silver and gold.

YOU WILL NEED

CHINESE LANTERNS

SCISSORS

ACRYLIC SIZE

FAKE GOLD LOOSE LEAF

ARTISTS' PAINTBRUSH

WARNING

Unripe Chinese lantern berries can be poisonous so please keep these decorations out of children's reach.

1

Spread out the five sepals that surround the Chinese lantern fruit and trim to neaten.

2

Paint each sepal with acrylic size and leave for a few minutes until it is clear.

3

Press on bits of the loose gold leaf all over the sepals.

4

With a dry paintbrush, brush off excess bits of the gold leaf and let the adorned fruits dry thoroughly before pushing into the tree's branches.

$\mathcal{C}$ANDLE HOLDERS

You can buy cookie cutters in a great number of shapes so why not make some star-shaped candle holders too?

YOU WILL NEED

SMALL CANDLES

FLORISTS' FOAM

HEART-SHAPED COOKIE CUTTER (LARGE ENOUGH FOR A CANDLE TO FIT COMFORTABLY INTO CENTER)

PAPER

WALLPAPER PASTE

ACRYLIC SIZE

ARTISTS' PAINTBRUSH

FAKE GOLD LOOSE LEAF

BRADAWL

CLOVES

1

Cut out a piece of florists' foam using the cutter, ensuring the foam is deeper than the candle. While still in the cutter, cut a hole from the foam that is slightly bigger than the candle.

2

Press the foam out of the cutter. Then paste strips of paper over the florists' foam using wallpaper paste. Allow to dry overnight.

3

Paint the heart with acrylic size and wait for a few minutes until it is clear.

4

Lie on pieces of the fake loose leaf gold, pressing it on with your fingers. Do this in a draught-free room.

5

Carefully and lightly brush off excess gold leaf using a dry paintbrush.

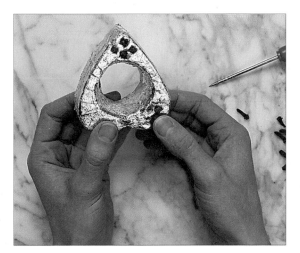

6

Poke holes for the cloves all around the holder using the bradawl. Then push the cloves into the holes ensuring they go in as far as possible.

7

Gently insert the candles, and the candleholders are now ready to be positioned at the foot of the tree. Do not leave unattended when lit.

GILDED POT

The finishing touch: parts of the pot showing through give it a more aged look.

1

Paint the pot with acrylic size. Paint well over the rim of the pot as this area will be very prominent. Allow the size to dry for a few minutes until it is clear.

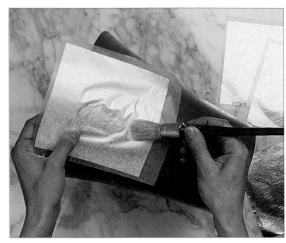

2

Press on sheets of gold transfer leaf using the stiff paintbrush.

3

Gently peel the backing off the transfer leaf. Don't worry if some of the terracotta shows through.

4

Brush off any excess bits with the same dry paintbrush.

Traditional Tree

Holly leaves with berries still attached and great swathes of ivy; handsome greens and vibrant reds interspersed with hints of gold: these elements are the essence of the traditionally decorated Christmas tree. But green and red alone, while a striking combination, need something to add a lift. Furthermore, as the texture of holly and ivy leaves is so similar to the pine tree itself, it is worth introducing other elements of texture. Here, this has been achieved by the gilded card star at the top of the tree and the charmingly unusual cherubs with their fluffy round tummies.

Many of the decorations on this tree can be made by children although little fingers should beware of the prickles on the holly. Finding the ingredients is always a good adventure and pulling ivy from tree trunks extraordinarily satisfying. The red baubles that are scattered all over the tree have been gathered from far and wide: a bauble here and a bauble there soon add up to a truly varied collection.

TRADITIONAL *Gallery*

Right: SUCH
SPLENDIDLY FAT
CHERUBS CAN'T HELP
BRINGING A SMILE TO
EVERYONE'S FACE AT
CHRISTMAS.

Below: THE ULTIMATE
IN TRADITIONAL
DECORATIONS: HOLLY
LEAVES WITH RED
BERRIES ARE GIVEN A
TOUCH OF GLAMOR
WITH THE AID OF A
GOLD PEN.

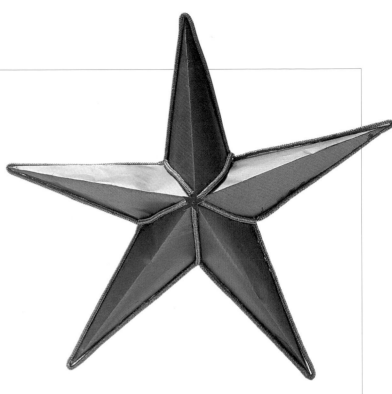

Above and right: THE HOLLY AND
THE IVY. THIS FESTIVE GREENERY
CAN BE USED ALONE, AS ABOVE,
OR COMBINED WITH MORE
ORNATE ADDITIONS, AS RIGHT.

Above right: TO CAP IT ALL, A
GOLD STAR DESIGNED TO LOOK
PERFECTLY HANDSOME ON TOP
OF A TRADITIONALLY DECORATED
CHRISTMAS TREE.

I VY GARLAND

Swathes of ivy and sprigs of holly can be quickly gathered from your garden or any nearby tract of woodland.

1

Wire together strands of trailing ivy using short lengths of the florists' wire.

2

Select some holly sprigs (variegated if you have it) and smooth on a blob of glitter from the glitter pen using your finger tips.

3

Paint some other holly sprigs with liquid leaf, applying it all over some of the leaves.

4

Wire the sprigs onto the ivy garland using the fake holly berries. If you can't find fake berries, wire together red beads in pairs.

HOLLY SPRIGS

Here is an incredibly quick and easy project that combines fresh holly leaves with fake berries.

YOU
WILL
NEED

HOLLY

LIQUID LEAF PAINT

ARTISTS' PAINTBRUSH

GOLD GLITTER PEN

FAKE HOLLY BERRIES

1

Paint some of the leaves of a sprig of holly with liquid leaf applying it with the artists' paintbrush.

2

Paint the remaining leaves using blobs of glitter from the glitter pen.

3

Paint some of the fake holly berries with the liquid leaf.

4

To complete each sprig, wire the fake berries onto the painted leaves.

GOLDEN STAR

Some very simple folds on gold paper and, presto, a golden star for the top of the tree is quickly created.

YOU WILL NEED

SCISSORS

GOLD CRAFT PAPER

CLEAR STICKY TAPE

ALL-PURPOSE GLUE

STIFF WHITE CARD

GOLD CORD

1 GOLD SEQUIN

1

Cut out five 4in (10cm) squares of gold craft paper. Fold each square in half diagonally and open out flat again.

2

On the reverse side, bring one corner to meet the center fold. Press flat, repeat on the other side and open out. Using the folds, make a 3-d shape overlapping the outside edges and securing with tape.

3

Repeat with each square of gold paper. Stick the bottom of each point onto a piece of stiff card butting them up close and placing a piece of sticky tape under the center points of the stars.

4

Cut out the star, trimming as close as possible to the gold paper.

5

Using the all-purpose glue, carefully stick the gold cord all the way around the edge of the star.

6

Finally, cut some short pieces of cord and stick over the joins of the points. For a neat finish, run the cord around to the back and stick a gold sequin onto the center front.

CONTENTED CHERUBS

The well-fed tummies of these cherubs are created from home-made pompoms: something that all children love to make.

YOU WILL NEED

TEMPLATES ON PAGE 125

WHITE CARD

GOLD LUREX THREAD

SCISSORS

GOLD PAPER

RUBBER-BASED GLUE

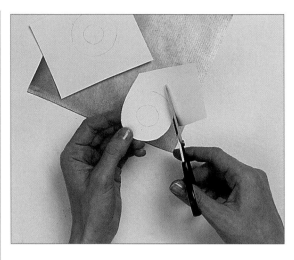

1

Using the template on page 125, cut out two circles of card. Then cut out the center from each one, also as indicated on the template on page 125.

2

With both circles of card together, wind several lengths of the lurex around and around until the card is completely covered and the central hole very small.

3

Running the point of the scissors between the two layers of card, snip the lurex.

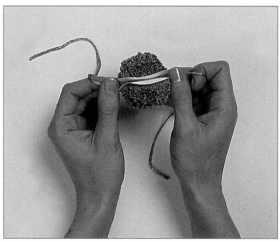

4

Tie a short length of lurex firmly around the center between the two layers of card. Tie the loose ends together to make a hanging loop. Cut the card circles away and fluff up the pompom.

5

Photocopy the templates on page 125 on the gold paper and cut out the head, arms and legs.

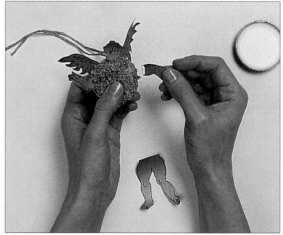

6

Using the rubber–based glue, stick each part of the body into the pompom. Ensure that the head stands in front of the hanging loop and then attach the rest of the body parts.

IVY WREATH

YOU WILL NEED

6 LONG PIECES OF IVY

ARTISTS' PAINTBRUSH

GOLD PAINT

16IN (40CM) OF FLORISTS' WIRE

CLEAR STICKY TAPE

GOLD SPRAY PAINT

6 CHILLIES

20 PEANUTS IN THEIR SHELLS

THIN GOLD CORD

1

Paint the leaves of three of the pieces of ivy with gold paint. Allow to dry.

2

Make a 6in (15cm) circle using the florists' wire doubled. Twist the ends around each other to secure. With clear tape, stick the pieces of ivy around the circle, one at a time, alternating gold and plain lengths.

3

Spray the chillies and peanuts very lightly with gold paint. The original color should still show in places.

4

With thin gold cord, tie the chillies by their stems and the peanuts around their middles to the wreath. Space them out and tie them on firmly.

 EMPLATES

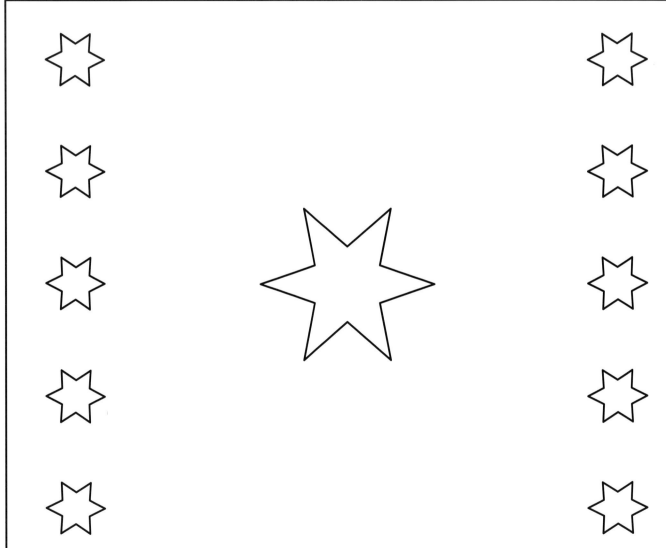

Templates

TRANSFERRING THE TEMPLATES

The outlines below or overleaf on pages 122-126 are all given at full size. To transfer them onto card or paper, use the following method:

• Trace the design onto tracing paper.

• Using a soft pencil, heavily draw over the lines on the reverse side of the tracing paper.

• Lay the tracing paper, right side up, onto the card or paper and draw over the design one more time. The pencil marks on the reverse of the paper will then be transferred to the card and paper ready for use.

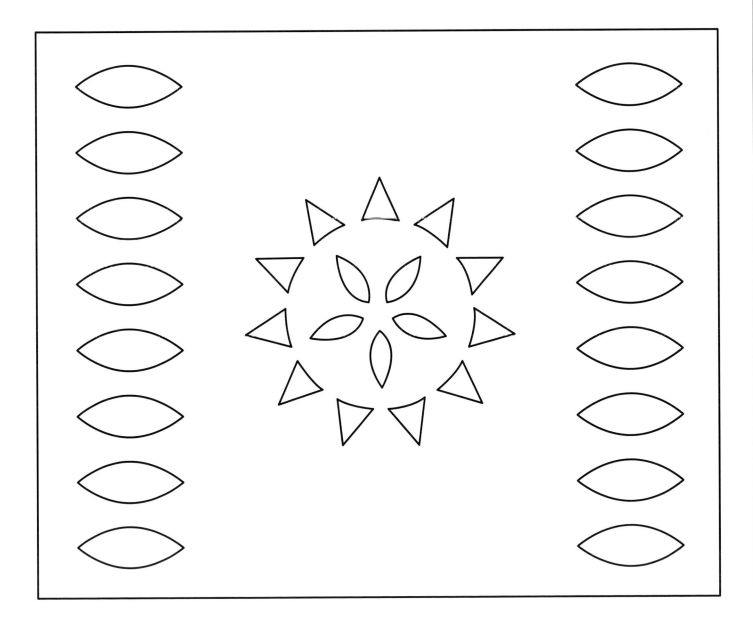

TIN ANGEL

See project on pages 84–87.

Wings (make 2)

Templates

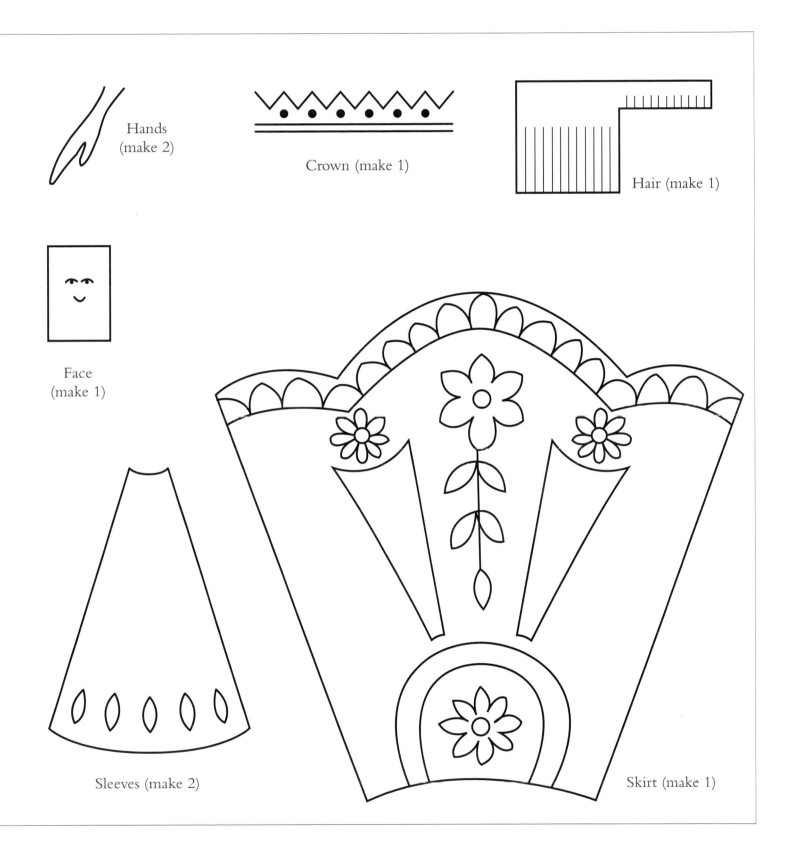

Hands
(make 2)

Crown (make 1)

Hair (make 1)

Face
(make 1)

Sleeves (make 2)

Skirt (make 1)

TIN STARS

FABRIC AND FELT STARS

See project on
pages 80–81

See projects on
pages 30–31 and
pages 66–67

 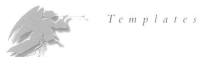 *Templates*

CONTENTED CHERUBS

See project on pages 116–117

Pompom circle
(cut out 2)

Head, arms and legs
(cut out 1 of each)

See project on pages 76-77

Templates

INDEX Page numbers in **bold** indicate photographs

AUTHOR'S ACKNOWLEDGEMENTS
The biggest thank you to Jacqui Hurst for taking many of the wonderful photographs in this book and for her help, ideas and pateince in having her house endlessly turned upside down. Thank you too, to Shona who took the pictures on pages 2 and 11 and all the step-by-step pictures with such care and enthusiasm; the team at Collins & Brown especially Kate Haxell for her patience, encouragement and hard work; Roger Daniels for his excellent design; Jennifer Tyndale, Roger Bristow and Cameron Brown who lent their beautiful houses for photography; to the Almanac Gallery for the use of their picture on page 2. Thank you to my Mum, Veronica, who from an early age encouraged us to make things wherever possible, and who I was able to call on at the drop of a hat in moments of crisis. Julie Daniel and Thomas, thank you for looking lovingly after Caspar while I was working on the book. Finally a huge thank you to Charlie for his constant help and encouragement and for never once complaining about our house being in a perpetual state of Christmas Eve.

ADDITIONAL PICTURE CREDITS
Page 2; card, Sheila Moxley © 1991, published courtesy of Roger la Borde UK. Page 8; Mary Evans Picture Library.

SPECIALIST MAIL-ORDER SUPPLIER OF ALUMINUM FOIL
Pyramid Art Suppliers
100 Paragon Parkway
Mansfield
Ohio 44903
call: (800) 6370955